Contents

Acknowledgements
Text by Ken Williams.
The publishers would like to thank
PowerGlide for their contribution to this

PowerGlide®
BILLIARDS & SNOOKER

Photographs on the inside covers and on
pages 1, 12, 22, 30, 41, 43 and 45
courtesy of Sporting Pictures (UK) Ltd.
All other photographs by Sylvio Dokov.
Illustrations by 1–11 line-art

Note Throughout the book players
are referred to individually as 'he'. This
should, of course, be taken to mean 'he
or she' where appropriate.

Introduction

The game of snooker continues to grow throughout the world. In *Know The Game Snooker* I have attempted to provide the beginner with the best possible advice and tuition to enable him to have a greater understanding of the techniques required. One player in a million has the ability to pot the ball with consummate ease, and for him the game will appear to be simple. But for the rest of us it is all a good deal more perplexing.

Sound technical advice is hard to come by at club level. With this in mind I have illustrated this book logically through all aspects of stance, cueing, cue-ball control and sound practice methods. Each of the shots illustrated is at the heart of snooker; learn them well and you will have a clearer insight into the game.

Always remember that to become an accomplished player you will have to devote many hours to practice. Understandably, most beginners just want to get on and play frames; after all, primarily snooker should be fun! However, if you neglect practice and do nothing but play, your cue-ball control technique will not develop as quickly as it should. Practise the various shots illustrated here in a competitive form with a playing partner and you will find it equally as entertaining as playing frames, and far more rewarding.

The author, Ken Williams ▶

The table

The bed of a standard full-size snooker table measures 12 ft × 6 ft 1½ in (3.66 m × 1.87 m), though this can vary slightly from manufacturer to manufacturer. It stands 2 ft 9½ in (85 cm) to 2 ft 10½ in (87.6 cm) from the floor. This slate bed is incorporated in an elaborate wooden frame, the bed being covered with a tightly stretched green woollen cloth (the 'baize'), which has a variable crop, termed the 'nap', running from the bottom (baulk) to the top (black spot) end of the table. There are six pockets, one at each corner and one exactly in the middle of each long side. Resilient rubber cushions, overhanging no more than 2 in (5.1 cm) and no less than 1½ in (3.8 cm), enclose the playing area. There is, of course, a gap in the cushion at each place where a pocket is situated, to allow the ball to enter.

A line is drawn across the width of the table parallel with the bottom cushion and 29 in (74 cm) from its face. This is called the 'baulk line'.

From the centre point of this line, a semi-circle is marked within the baulk area with a radius of 11½ in (29 cm). This is called the 'D'. When the player is 'in hand' – that is, when his cue ball is off the table or after it has entered a pocket – he must take his next stroke from the 'D' area. Any point may be chosen, either on the baulk line or within the semi-circular area.

The other markings consist of four spots on the imaginary central longitudinal line of the table. These spots, marked with very small wafer-like pieces of silk, or by tailor's chalk, are positioned as follows:

- at the centre of the baulk line
- at the centre of the table itself (the centre spot')
- halfway between the centre spot and the face of the top cushion (the 'pyramid spot')
- 12¾ in (32.4 cm) from the face of the top cushion (the 'spot')
- the semi-circle 'D' describes from the green to the yellow spot.

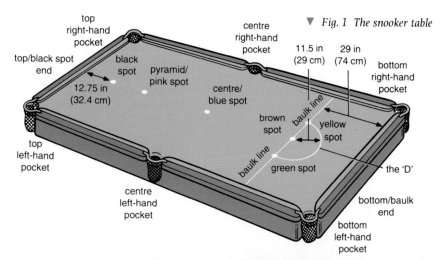

▼ *Fig. 1 The snooker table*

Care of the table

The table should be brushed with a special table brush either before or after each day's play. Brush firmly but not vigorously since there is little point in sending dust or dirt into the air only for it to settle on the table again.

Always brush from the baulk end towards the black spot end, i.e. with the nap. Brush in straight lines so that dust and dirt are neatly gathered under the top cushion. Then, with the top of the brush sweep the accumulated dust gently into one of the pockets, shaking the latter immediately to make sure that the dust does not settle there.

When brushing has been completed, it is a good idea to draw a baize-covered pad in long continuous straight strokes up the table to prepare the cloth for ironing.

Ironing should be done with a special iron which should be tested for heat before applying it to the cloth. When you judge the iron to be ready, place it briefly on a piece of newspaper. If the paper discolours, even slightly, the iron is too hot. If, however, there is no fear of burning the cloth, draw the iron in long continuous straight strokes up the table, holding it at a slight angle to the cushions and without coming into contact with them. Remember, cushions are made of rubber!

A valuable tip: when placing any of the coloured balls on the spots, always place it to one side of the spot and slide it into place. Banging a ball down on a spot merely creates a slight hole in the cloth.

After play, the table should always be covered with a light sheet, available from all recognised snooker stockists.

Balls

When playing on a full-size table, snooker balls must be $2\frac{1}{16}$ in (5.25 cm) in diameter. Smaller sizes are available for small tables.

Care of the balls

Avoid keeping balls in extremely hot or extremely cold conditions. Keeping the balls clean is absolutely crucial. Before playing, it is a good idea to wipe the balls with a damp cloth and polish them dry with a dry cloth. Failing this, always make sure that the cue ball is clean before the start of each frame. The longer that balls are used without cleaning, the more likely it is that spots of dirt and chalk will become ingrained and affect their performance.

Occasionally, one set of balls will become muddled with another. This is particularly serious if the cue ball is either heavier or lighter than the other balls. In either case, the angles at which the cue ball rebounds from other balls will be affected. If heavier, the cue ball will run through the contacted object ball; if lighter, it will spring wider.

The cue

The snooker cue is a sophisticated piece of equipment and the most important part of your armoury. Before you buy a cue of your own you will have to make do with a cue from the communal rack at the club where you play. The best cue is the one that allows you to perform the various functions demanded of it.

Most cues are produced to a standard length of 4 ft 10 in (147 cm), and as such these cues for the most part are adequate. However, bear in mind that a length of approximately 4 ft 8½ in (143 cm) does produce a more powerful cue.

The most popular material for the shaft of the cue is straight-grained ash. The grain should not be too wide: about ten grain lines to the inch (four to the centimetre) looks good and is sufficient to promote the required shaft strength. Maple is also a perfectly good material, but because of its density it does tend to push the cue ball off the intended line when 'side' is applied. In my experience a cue tip size of 0.38 in (9.75 mm) allows the ball to hold its intended line more accurately. (The tip size required also depends on the actual stress strength of the particular piece of timber used in the cue.)

The popular weight for a cue is between 17 oz (482 g) and 17½ oz (496 g), with the weight balancing forwards when the cue is suspended on the finger at the top of the butt splicing. The forward weight in the shaft is the key to a well-balanced and correctly powered cue. A cue that is over-weighted to the back tends to rise off the bridge during the execution of the stroke.

Cues are made in one-, two- and three-piece models, either hand made or machine spliced. Modern two-piece cue joints are now very dependable.

Fitting and shaping a new cue tip

Always choose the best quality tip available. Various types are on the market. Select the tip that has the appropriate texture and hardness, i.e. not too hard, not too soft. A Blue Elk style tip is by far the most popular choice for top-class players.

Fitting your tip is relatively easy provided that you have the appropriate equipment.

● First clean and level the brass ferrule and wood with a cue ferrule leveller.
● Rub the base of the cue tip on a piece of fine sandpaper to remove any tip dressing. Make sure the tip is perfectly flat and level.
● Apply a top quality instant tip adhesive and position the tip. Apply pressure with the thumb for about ten seconds. Set aside for a few minutes before trimming and shaping. If an oversize tip is used, turn the cue on to the tip and trim with a sharp blade.

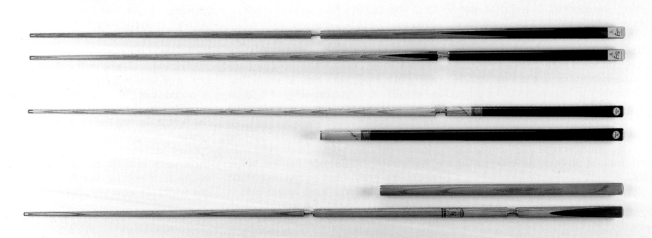

▲ *Cues*

▲ *Cue tip shaper*

0.35 in (9 mm)   0.39 in (10 mm)   0.43 in (11 mm)

actual size

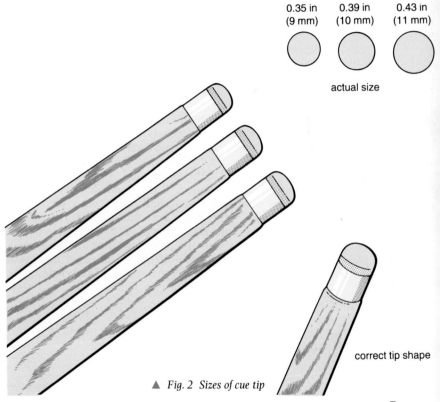

correct tip shape

▲ *Fig. 2 Sizes of cue tip*

Chalking the cue tip

The act of chalking the cue tip is not treated with a great deal of reverence by the large majority of snooker players. All players are aware that chalk helps to eliminate mis-cues, but there are other reasons why chalking is so critical.

I cannot emphasise enough the importance of using a good quality billiards chalk. It must be of the correct grit and make-up – too hard and the chalk will not adhere to the cue tip, too soft and powdery and it will stick to the ball and foul the cloth. The latter is one of the major reasons for what are commonly referred to as 'kicks' – the cue ball acting in a completely opposite way to the intention when the shot was played. Equally, the cue tip must be of a fibre make-up to receive the chalk. If the tip is too hard the chalk will not adhere, and if it is too soft the fibres will break up, preventing a proper feel between cue tip and ball.

The act of applying the chalk to the tip is something not to be overlooked. The chalk should be held in either hand in a stationary position at a slight angle. When the cue is rotated, this action tends to shape the top half of the tip correctly. The chalk should never be *scrubbed* on to the tip. Used correctly, the chalk will form a tidy hole in its top. It is a good idea to rub the face of the chalk block on a piece of sandpaper from time to time. This takes the side of the chalk down at the same pace as the hole, avoiding the disastrous rubbing of the chalk edges against the lower part of the brass ferrule.

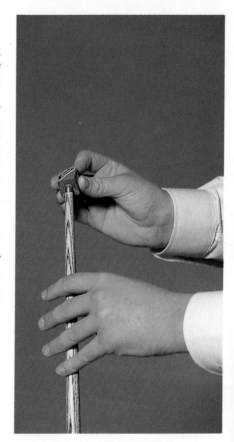

Chalking the cue tip ▶

The rests

Various designs of cue rests are available to assist you in those awkward locations where it is not possible to reach with your normal stance. A metal or plastic cross at the end of the rest forms a bridge, and different lengths of rest are available. The short, or 'half-butt', rest is 8 ft (2.4 m) long, while the 'long rest' is 12 ft (3.6 m) long. A long cue is provided for each of these rests.

There are also positions in which the player cannot easily contact his cue ball because another ball is close to it. To cope with this difficulty, the player uses the 'spider' rest, providing a bridge of extra height with a long handle like the other rests.

The development of the modern integrated cue and extension allows the player to extend his own cue as may be necessary, making life more comfortable.

The rests ▶

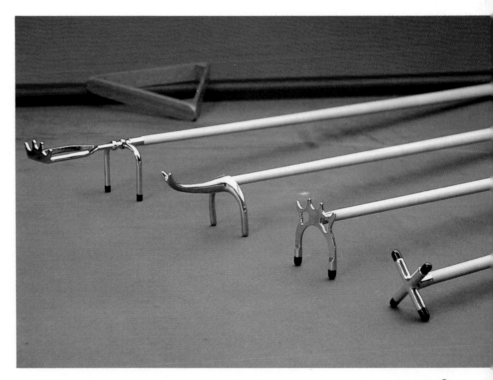

9

Accessories

You would be well advised to choose with some care the other items you may need since many accessories are available to the enthusiast, some good and some not so good.

A cue case to accompany your cue is more important than some other accessories on the market. Cue cases are available in one-, two- and three-piece models. Quality can vary dramatically, depending on the price.

A variety of utility items are available to you in the form of chalk cubes, tips, tip adhesives, tip shapers, ferrule levellers, cue cleaners and silicon polishes. Choose the best quality accessories you can afford because it makes good sense in the long term.

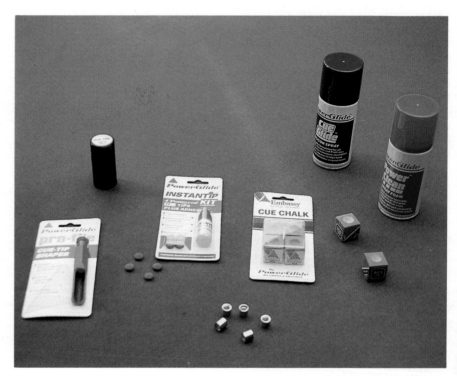

Accessories ▶

The game

Snooker uses 22 balls. These are:

- the cue ball (white), which each player uses in turn
- 15 red balls (value = 1 point each)
- the yellow ball (2 points)
- the green ball (3)
- the brown ball (4)
- the blue ball (5)
- the pink ball (6)
- the black ball (7).

The yellow, green, brown, blue, pink and black balls are known collectively as 'the colours' and are listed above in order of rotation. Any of the colours may be potted after the potting of a red ball. When all of the reds have been potted, the colours must be potted in the above named rotation.

The balls are placed in the manner shown in fig. 3. The 15 red balls form a pyramid or triangular pack (hence the expression 'to break the pack', to disturb the opening formation of red balls). A triangular wooden frame – the 'triangle' – enables the reds to be set up in this way. The apex red should be as near as possible to the pink ball without touching it. The six colours are located on their respective spots as shown.

The object of the game is to pot all the balls in succession, as follows. A red ball is potted first, then any colour, then another red, then a colour, and so on until all 15 reds are pocketed. The reds remain in the pocket each time they are potted, but a colour is retrieved from the pocket and replaced on its own spot each time.

After all the red balls have been cleared from the table, the six colours remain. These must be potted in the aforementioned order of rotation. After the black ball is potted, the game is finished. The winner is the player who gains the higher number of points.

Such a game is called a 'frame' (of snooker), and a match consists of a given number of frames which may be anything from 'the best of three frames' up to something like 'the best of 37 frames'.

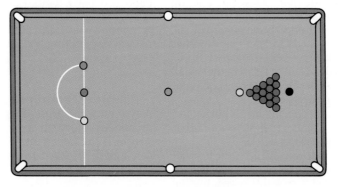

▲ *Fig. 3 The position of the balls*

11

Fouls

A player must not:

- *push* the cue ball with the cue, instead of *striking* it
- force a ball (or balls) off the table
- play a stroke with both feet off the ground
- play a stroke before the balls have come to rest
- touch the ball other than with the cue tip, e.g. with his hand or his clothes
- touch the ball with the cue tip before he has delivered his stroke
- use the 'jump shot', by which the cue ball is made to leap over another ball by hitting it very low down
- use a dead ball to test whether a ball will pass another, or go on a spot, or for any other purpose
- direct the cue ball into a pocket ('to go in-off') whether it strikes another ball or balls or not
- pot a ball out of the correct order (i.e. pot one that is not on), e.g. by potting one red then another red, instead of a colour

- fail to hit the ball he has nominated after a foul by his opponent
- move a ball which is touching the cue ball, instead of playing away from it without moving it
- strike two balls simultaneously unless both are red balls, or one is the ball nominated and the other is the ball on
- 'snooker' (*see* later) with the ball nominated after a foul, unless only pink and black balls remain on the table
- commit a foul after potting a red ball before nominating or attempting to play a colour. The penalty is seven points.

After a foul stroke by his opponent, a player may play from the position left, or ask his opponent to play the next stroke. If the opponent fails again, he can again be asked to play the next stroke.

Using the rest ▶

12

Penalties

The penalties for the various fouls are given in the official rule book, obtainable from the World Professional Billiards and Snooker Association, 27 Oakfield Road, Clifton, Bristol BS8 2AT. As a general principle, the penalties for most fouls are calculated according to the values of the balls involved in the foul, and the player forfeits the value of the highest.

As the minimum penalty is four points, it follows that the forfeit value of the red, yellow and green balls will be four in each case, not one, two and three respectively.

There is also a rule stating that the first impact governs all strokes, but this does not always apply if two fouls are involved in the stroke.

Here are some examples.

● A player on red strikes black – seven points forfeit (or, as is commonly said, 'seven away').
● A player on black strikes red – seven points forfeit. Both here and in the above example the black value – seven – is the higher and therefore determines the forfeit.
● A player on red strikes blue – five away. The blue value – five – is higher than the red forfeit value – four.
● A player on blue strikes green. The cue ball, still moving, contacts pink which enters a pocket, and the player then fouls black with his cue. In this case the forfeit is seven.
● A player pots yellow, and then fouls pink with his cue after the cue ball has stopped. The penalty is six points, and the yellow is re-spotted.
● A player 'snookers' (*see* later) with the nominated ball (free ball). The penalty is the value of the ball on. Therefore, if the player chooses black as his nominated ball after a foul, when the green is on, and he then snookers with the black, his penalty is only four points.
● Black is the ball on, but after the player has hit it, it cannons on to the blue and pots it. The penalty is seven points, the highest value involved.
● A player is on a red and he hits it, but his cue ball goes on to strike black and then goes into a pocket. The penalty is four points – the first impact (which governs all strokes) was on the red, for which the penalty is the minimum, four.
● A player on red is snookered after a foul. He nominates black, fails to hit it, and strikes a red, also potting black. The penalty is four points because black – the nominated ball – acquires the value of the red for which it was nominated, and therefore also acquires its penalty value.

General strategy

The chief aim, of course, is to pot as many balls as possible in order to win frames and thus the game. Interweaved with the potting, what are termed 'snookers' can be played by positioning the cue ball behind a colour, thus blocking its path to the next ball 'on', i.e. any red ball or, in the case of the colours, the ball left on the table that is of the lowest value.

Positional play is all important, and standard playing techniques have been well documented. In the following pages I will demonstrate the most important ways to play them.

The stance

It must be made abundantly clear at the outset that the sighting of the cue ball has no bearing whatsoever on the actual cueing action. It is a part of sighting 'parallax'. The overall sighting discipline is dealt with on page 18.

Position A – placing the feet and legs

In my opinion there is no single, concrete, set position for the feet relative to the cue-arm position as depicted in the photograph of position A on the opposite page. In the case of the right-handed player, the right foot, by degree, can be placed in various positions from player to player, i.e. dead in line, inside or outside the vertical cue arm. This is because it positively affects the follow-through line of the cue after contact with the cue ball. After the follow-through, if the cue finishes to the left of the follow-through line the shot will almost certainly be missed to the right of the target pocket. Conversely, if the cue finishes to the right of the follow-through line the shot will be missed to the left of the target pocket.

With these facts clear in your mind, experiment with various foot positions until the correct follow-through line is mastered. It is imperative that you do not attempt to correct your follow-through in mid-action. Your action should be part of a committed discipline, perfectly smooth and relaxed.

Having decided the most effective leg and foot position, the opposite leg should be place in a firm-set, comfortable position with the leg bent and slightly forward. The back leg should be approximately 5° back of vertical, but not stretched (see the main photograph opposite). The inset shows the right leg forwards of vertical – this is incorrect. Note that if the leg is kept in the vertical position, it does tend to stop the body getting into a correct, flat-plain position – hence the back leg angle.

The importance of the cue-arm position is explained on page 17.

Study 'The straight pot' on page 29 for a visual explanation of the cause and effect of cue deviation from the straight line.

If you aspire to playing good snooker, the following disciplines are absolutely essential.

- The stance is the actual standing position – position A . . .
- coupled with elbow–foot alignment – position B . . .
- and the movement of the cue arm – position C.

POSITION A Main photo: there is ▶ no single, concrete, set position for the feet relative to the cue-arm position – just concentrate on mastering the correct follow-through line. Inset: however, the right leg here is forwards of the vertical, something to be avoided

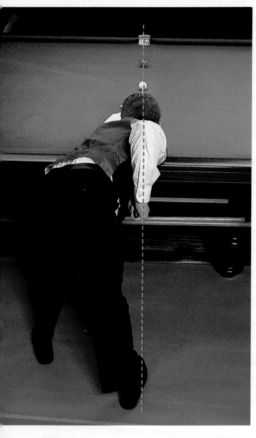

Position B – aligning the elbow vertically

The photograph on the left shows clearly all the ingredients of an ideal cue action stance.

● The elbow point coupled with a vertical cue aim. The elbow point should pivot consistently from a set position whenever possible. The pivot swing needs only to be as long as is necessary to produce the power required for any shot, i.e. if it is a long stun shot it will require a longer swing than a short stun shot. This variable swing technique should be developed to enable greater sophistication of cue delivery.

● The position of hand and wrist relative to the cue delivery line. The cue should be gripped ideally in a soft but firm manner, and the wrist should not be floppy.

● The angle of the feet also relative to the cue line. Obviously, this could be a contentious point since some top professionals use the parallel method while others set the foot off at a small angle. It is a certain fact that setting the feet parallel to the cue line can have the effect of straightening the cue's follow-through. The decision is yours. Experiment until you find what's best for you.

Unless all of these important aspects of the stance and cue action gel together, consistent play of a very high standard is impossible.

◀ *POSITION B   The cue action*

Position C – the movement of the cue arm

In the case of the cue arm, it is of paramount importance that it should be vertical, as in position C in the photograph on the right, and that it should pivot at the apex of the elbow point with a controlled swing length roughly equal backwards and forwards of the fixed apex point. Ideally, it should only be long enough to generate the power required to play any particular shot.

Over-swinging, which may be intended to produce more power, should be avoided if at all possible since the elbow pivot point will almost certainly be unlocked, and the cue arm thrown off its true line. Unless a player happens to possess a very naturally straight action, using too much power almost inevitably results in an inaccurate delivery of the cue.

Probably the single most important principle in delivering the cue correctly is to keep as still as possible. Keep your head down during the shot because if your head moves the cue tip will move

and, in turn, you will not strike your predetermined cue-ball contact point, resulting in the inevitably bad positional shot.

Remember – the most difficult and crucial task is to hit the pre-determined contact point on the cue ball.

The cueing discipline is all important – the same stance and cueing action should be effected on every shot that you play. No matter how accurately you judge the 'shot on', it could prove to be to no avail if you do not deliver the cue tip to its intended target on the cue ball.

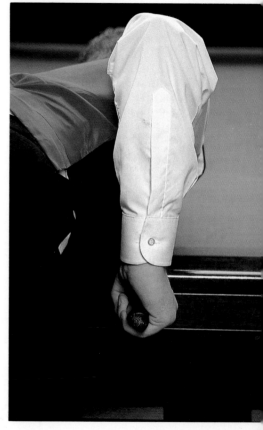

POSITION C The cue arm ▶

17

Sighting

Any player who from the outset pots the ball with consummate ease is very fortunate indeed, since the vast majority of us are not so lucky. True sighting is primarily a gift. Three methods of sighting apply.

● Photograph A shows the classical centre two-eyed style – arguably the truest method of sighting since it is a perfect natural parallax. Correct parallax depends on sighting down the line of the cue that is equal left and right. Incorrect parallax leads to distortion of sighting which causes the unintended application of side.

● Photograph B illustrates a left-eye sighting. The left eye is dominant and the right eye plays very little part, i.e. the parallax does not apply.

● Photograph C illustrates the same sighting method but using the right as the dominant eye.

Each of these three methods is fine until the eye–cue relationship falters, i.e. moves out of direct line with the cue and settles somewhere between the pupil of the eye and the bridge of the nose. The resulting effect is an unbalanced parallax which in turn impairs your ability to sight the centre of the

▲ *(A) Classical centre two-eyed stance*   ▲ *(B) Left-eye sighting*

cue ball accurately. This means that what you see as the centre is not the centre, resulting in an unintended application of side.

▲ *(C) Right-eye sighting*

The feet

The positioning of the feet could well be the controlling feature that enables accurate straight line potting.

Either by natural means or by a conscious decision, a number of professionals place the right back foot (if a right-handed player) straight down the cue line as referred to on page 14.

The two photographs on the right serve only to show the two techniques clearly. It doesn't matter which position you choose, as long as it is effective for you. Having said this, it is as well to know how you can correct your follow-through if necessary, rather than carrying on for years not knowing how to put matters right.

▲ *Back foot aligned with cue line*

Back foot out to the right ▶

The bridge

The forming of the bridge hand and its grip on the cloth is undoubtedly as important as any other facet of cueing discipline.

Ideally, the bridge should be formed with the knuckles of the hand raised into a fairly high position, with the fingers firmly out and spread wide, enabling you to grip the cloth firmly.

Naturally enough, bridge hands vary dramatically and, to be fair, it is not that important what shape it takes as long as it adheres to the basic criteria. A soft, floppy bridge hand will definitely be a handicap to your game. If you find that your bridge hand is floppy, practise flexing the bridge and fingers on a firm surface when not actually playing.

Don't let awkward bridging throw you. Various hand positions can be adopted for getting over the top of balls, for bridging off the cushion, and for screwing the ball with the dropped bridge thumb – *see* the following photographs. Be versatile. Develop your own technique.

20

▲ *Orthodox bridge*

▲ *Bridge hand incorrect – too sloppy*

Right   *Elevating the bridge*

Far right   *Bridging on the cushion*

Right   *Bridging along the side edge of the cushion*

Far right   *Bridging along the cushion from near the jaws of a pocket*

The bridge arm

It would be understandable if the beginner was a little confused as to which bridge arm position is correct. My own preference is to extend the arm in such a way that it is thrust out from the shoulder as straight as possible. But it is still relaxed and comfortable.

In some cases the taller player finds it easier to bend the arm slightly to such a degree that his sighting of the cue ball is not impaired.

As a guide, it is probably prudent to base your style on a first-class cueist from the professional ranks. Having said this, what comes naturally will normally work well enough. If it *does* work, stay with it.

◄ *Placing the bridge arm is not an exact science, but try to extend it so that it is as straight as possible in relation to the shoulder*

Striking
the plain ball

Plain ball striking should be, without doubt, the prime ingredient in your playing technique. If a player is good enough to attain perfect position on every shot played, it probably would not be necessary to use any other shot method. Since such a standard is highly unlikely, plain ball striking is the only way that you can tell if you are sighting the cue ball accurately.

Players missing simple shots tend to blame misjudgement of the angle as the reason for the missed shot. The fact is, judgement of the shot angle is actually the one fact you can take for granted. Almost all missed shots are caused either by not striking the dead centre of the cue ball (*see* fig. 4), i.e. applying unintended or intended side, or by the effects of the cloth nap.

Quite naturally, your cue action should never be far from your thoughts, and is an integral part of accurate plain ball striking.

The long straight pot as described on page 29 will show up your sighting and cueing indiscretions better than any other method of practice.

▼ *Fig. 4 Striking the plain ball*

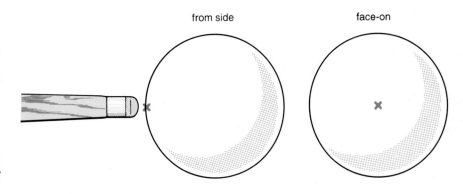

from side   face-on

Top-spin

Players in general think that top-spin (or 'top') is generated by striking the cue ball approximately $\frac{1}{2}$ in (1 cm) from the top. The fact is, a cue ball contact at any point above the plain ball (dead centre) imparts a varying degree of top, and should be treated accordingly (*see* fig. 5).

Although top of any degree is generally thought of as simple, nothing could be further from the truth. Unfortunately, any shot played this way is very prone to the effects of unintended applied side.

It is of paramount importance to play any run-through shot with the cue on a level plain. Therefore, you must raise or lower the bridge hand according to the height of the contact point required. A sweet, controlled stroke is the undeniable secret.

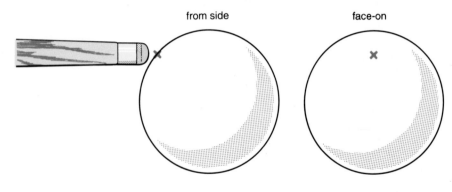

from side   face-on

▲ *Fig. 5 Playing with top*

Side

Playing with side creates significantly more problems for the novice than any other aspect of cue-ball control. However, this is not to say that it is such a difficult principle to understand, so long as you take time to analyse the momentum and path of the cue ball. Every shot you play when using side will squeeze the cue ball in the opposite direction to which the side is applied.

When playing with side, an accepted playing position of 12–18 in (30–45 cm) from the object ball is ideal – any further away and the spin on the cue ball will start to take effect and the cue ball will come back to the side to which the side was applied. It is essential that the shot is played with sufficient forward momentum to ensure that the cue ball deviates to the smallest extent possible from the straight path of cue ball to object ball. This extent must be allowed for when assessing any particular shot.

The influence of the 'shaft power' of the cue is of considerable importance,

and is referred to on page 5. Practise a shot that will help you to discover and observe the effect of side impact deviation.

▼ *Fig. 6 Playing with side*

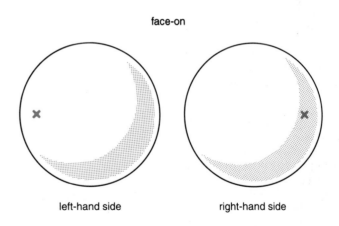

face-on

left-hand side   right-hand side

The screw shot

Almost without exception, the novice has great difficulty with the screw shot. There are various reasons why this is so.

● Obviously, there is the prime requirement to strike the lower part of the cue ball.
● It is essential that the player has a good quality cue tip, correctly shaped, coupled with a smooth cue action.
● What defines screw? Players often say, 'I can't screw the ball.' My reply is, 'Of course you can. You've simply got to strike the spot on the cue ball you aim at.' The major requirement in your cueing discipline is to keep the body still and the head down. If you try to employ too much power in an attempt to screw the ball long distances, you will almost certainly lift your head. Consequently, the cue tip will rise with you, resulting nearly always in you only screwing the cue ball a couple of inches. Here lies the answer – use the same, firm power on each shot.

● Strike the cue ball as shown in fig. 7. Do not expect to screw the ball at best more than 2–3 ft (60–90 cm). Screwing the cue ball long distances requires a good cue action, a good tip, and a fast bed cloth.

● Practise striking the cue ball in various positions at 1 mm variants up the ball, and let the point that you strike effectively make the difference you require in your screwing distance.

▼ *Fig. 7 Playing with screw*

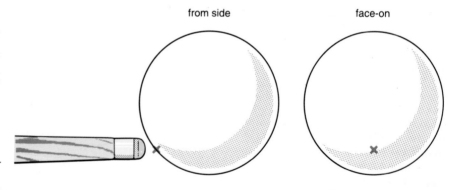

from side   face-on

The swerve shot

When playing a swerve shot, raise the bridge on to the tips of your fingers to a position which allows you to attack the cue ball from above. Using a downward action, strike the cue ball at approximately one o'clock when using right-hand side, and at eleven o'clock when using left-hand side. Take particular note of the path of the cue ball during its first forward motion, i.e. initially to the left when applying right-hand side, and conversely to the right when applying left-hand side.

Fig. 8 shows clearly what you need to understand in order to apply swerve successfully.

The swerve shot has never been a particularly accurate means of positional play due to the various speeds at which it can be played. But it is obviously a useful shot and is well worth practising.

Fig. 8 Playing with swerve ▶

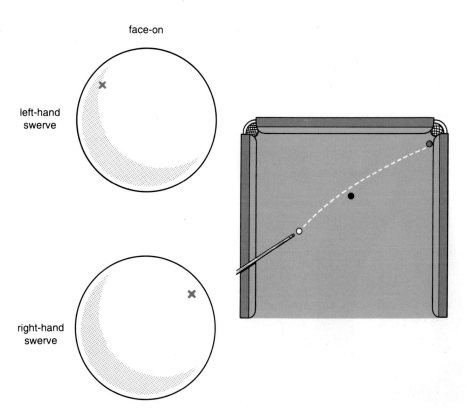

face-on

left-hand
swerve

right-hand
swerve

The stun run-through

The practice stun run-through is really quite simple. Place the cue ball and object ball 12–18 in (30–45 cm) apart. Aim the cue tip to the dead centre of the cue ball (point A in fig. 9), and punch firmly (do not roll the ball). After contact, the cue ball will travel forwards approximately 3 in (8 cm).

This will happen each time you play this type of shot. Varying the point where the tip strikes the cue ball – try 1 mm variants as in points B and C – will send the cue ball varying distances forwards after contact with the object ball.

Keep your cueing discipline in the back of your mind at all times.

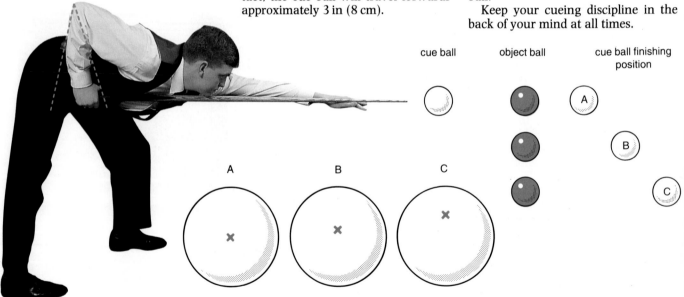

▲ *Fig. 9 The stun run-through*

The straight pot

Probably the single most important reason for missing the straight pot is incorrect sighting of the cue ball, i.e. not seeing the centre contact point. You may think that you are seeing it, but if your chin is right or left of the centre of the cue shaft, your parallax must be wrong in relation to the cue shaft line (*see* page 18). The subsequent visual adjustment means that you will adjust the tip to the centre as you see it! At this point you may not be right in your assumption. Refer to the stance discipline on pages 14–17 to refresh your memory about this phenomenon.

Fig. 10 shows the effect of an incorrect follow-through. Struck left of centre, cue ball A will squeeze to the right and the object ball will miss the pocket to the left; vice versa for cue ball B. Stop and think about it – it is totally logical.

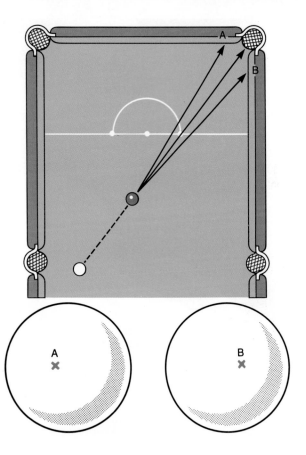

Fig. 10 The straight pot ▶

29

How to practise

Cue-ball control

Each of the practice shots illustrated on the following pages is intended to give you an insight into what can be achieved.

If it is your intention to turn yourself into an accomplished player, then the stance and cueing disciplines are of paramount importance.

Remember, on every shot you play:

The discipline

K – Know
Y – Your
D – Discipline.

◀ *Maintain your concentration!*

Mid-table cue-ball control (1)

Place the blue ball on to the centre spot, placing the cue ball at a slight angle to the blue ball (as illustrated in fig. 11) approximately 12–15 in (30–40 cm) away. Set any three balls in a line across the table around the pink spot. Strike the cue ball as shown on positions A, B and C, and note carefully the different angles produced. Play it as a *punch* shot.

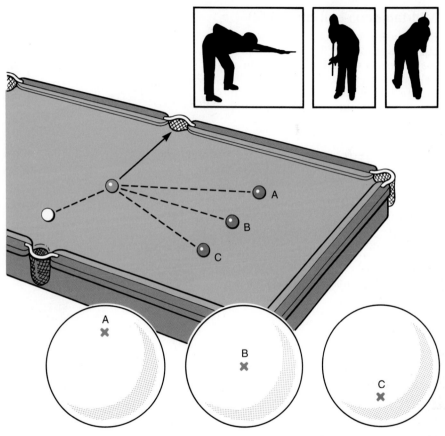

Fig. 11 Practising mid-table cue-ball ▶
control (1)

Mid-table cue-ball control (2)

Place the black ball on its spot. Set the cue ball as shown in fig. 12 on to a pre-marked chalk mark. Position any three balls as shown in the illustration. Strike the cue ball in positions A, B and C to pot the black and obtain positional contact on the three balls.

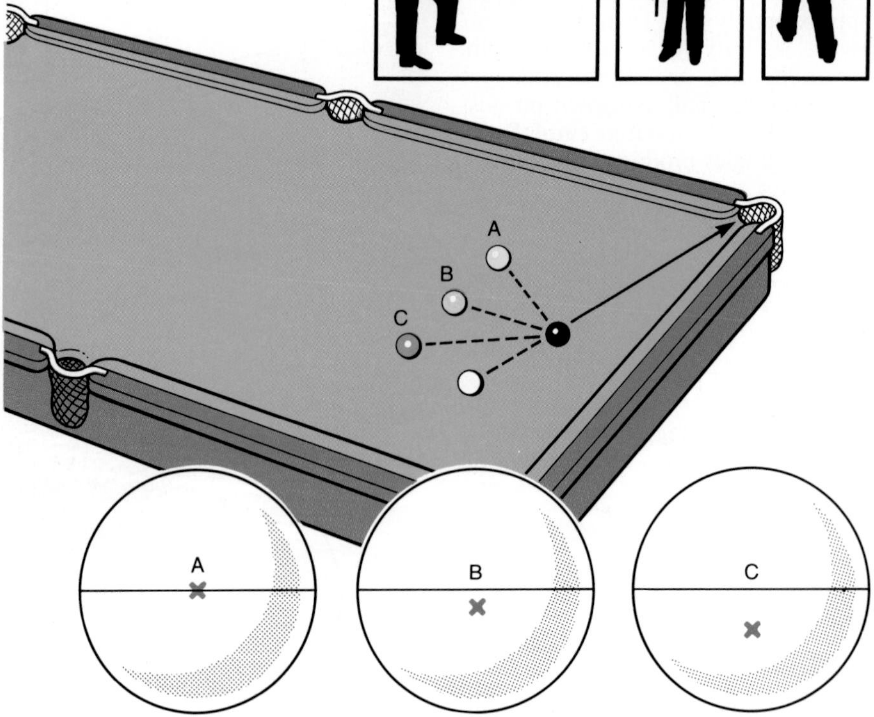

Fig. 12 Practising mid-table cue-ball ▶
control (2)

Dislodging balls
from the cushion

Practise this shot by placing the cue ball on a predetermined mark on the table as in the previous drill. Place three balls along the side cushion. Strike the cue ball on the positions marked A, B and C in potting the black and play as a punch shot with medium power. This is a first-class shot in learning the action of stun and cue-ball swing. Play it as a punch shot.

Fig. 13 Practising dislodging balls from ▶
the cushion

The stun off the cushion

This shot is one of the most important shots to practise because a player will be confronted frequently with an object ball near the top cushion. Place the cue ball in position X as shown in fig. 14. Play it as a plain ball shot at various points up the centre line of the cue ball, marked A, B, C and D, to strike the red. This shot can be played in ways that will achieve many finishing positions of the cue ball when playing for position on the black, and is valuable in improving your knowledge of cue-ball control. Play it as a punch shot.

Depending on when the cue-ball angle narrows in relation to the cushion, study fig. 15 on the opposite page for optional shots of a follow-through with side and top. In either case, do not let the object ball touch the cushion prior to entering the pocket.

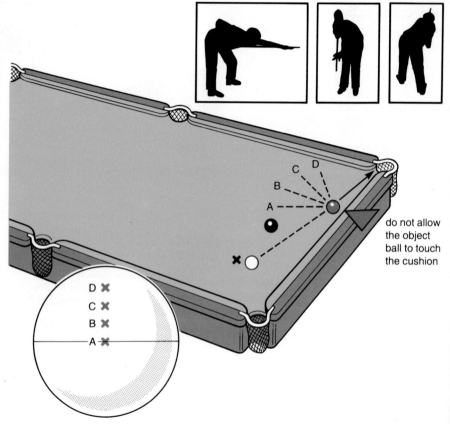

do not allow the object ball to touch the cushion

Fig. 14 Practising the stun off the ▶
cushion

Running side

Shot A and shot B in fig. 15 are the optional shots to the stun off the cushion, and the same technique is used on both shots. When the potting line is narrow in relation to the pocket opening, the shot should be played with top and running side, as shown on the cue ball in the illustration. With shot A the cue ball is closer to the cushion than is the object ball. Play with running side so that the cue ball strikes the side cushion and obtains position on the black. **Do allow, although only marginally, for the squeeze created by the applied side of the cue ball to the right**. In other words, your target point should be to the right of the pocket opening. With shot B the cue ball is further from the cushion than is the object ball. The line of follow-through is on to the top cushion, to the side cushion, and into position on the black.

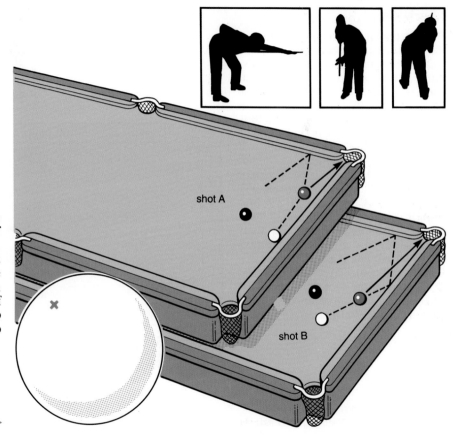

Fig. 15 Practising running side ▶

Check side

This particular shot is very important when clearing the colours.

Note the object ball 'target allowance' when accessing this shot. In effect, the cue ball is squeezed by the applied left-hand side which creates a thinner contact on the object ball; thus the shot is affected. It must be played firmly, otherwise the cue ball will swing to some degree back to the left and the shot could be missed. The pace with which the cue ball is struck will determine that the cue ball will first strike the right-hand cushion, return to the left-hand cushion, and then travel to a point where good position on the brown ball is attained.

Play with left-hand side and top. Avoid playing the shot slowly because otherwise it is almost impossible to keep the ball on the desired path.

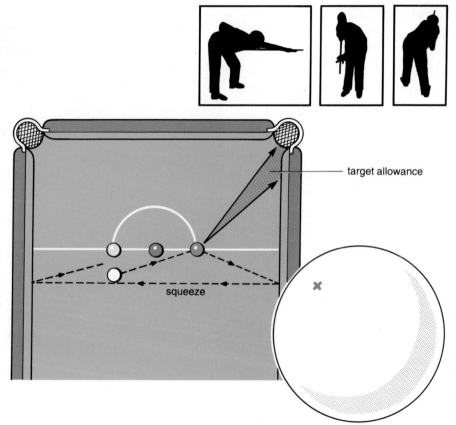

target allowance

squeeze

Fig. 16 Practising check side ▶

Other important shots

The break

The important principle to remember when breaking off is to make allowance for the 'push' that the applied right-hand side contact of the cue ball promotes. The target point should be the end red (A in fig. 17). The effect of the right-hand side will 'push' the cue ball over to make contact with the penultimate red, thus allowing the path of the cue ball as shown.

Do not play the shot slowly because this would have the effect of 'swerve' to the right, resulting in thin contact of the end red or even a complete miss. Play the break as a firm punch with follow-through.

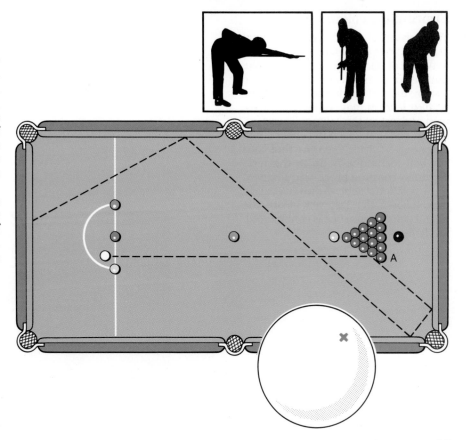

Fig. 17 The break ▶

Clearing the colours

The potting of the colours is a vital aspect of any match because the majority of games are decided by the number of points accumulated on the last six balls of the frame. Even at the highest level of play, many games are won and lost on the colours. Therefore, it is crucial that, given the opportunity to score, you strive to ensure that your cue-ball technique is up to the task. Arguably the most precise requirement is the positional shot off the final colour that follows the last red before the actual colour sequence is commenced. Study figs 18–23.

Yellow

A full three-quarter-ball angle contact on the yellow allows the opportunity to play a firm stun shot (without the cue ball touching the cusion) on to the green. (*See* fig. 18.)

▼ *Fig. 18*

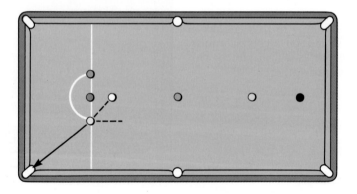

Green

A three-quarter-ball angle on the green with a firm stun should ideally leave a half-ball contact on the brown, without the cue ball touching the cushion. (*See* fig. 19.)

Brown

A half-ball contact on the brown should allow a natural stun on the side cushion, leaving a three-quarter-ball contact on the blue. Take care to prevent the cue ball from drifting to the lower side of the blue ball because this would mean a difficult power shot round the table to obtain position on the pink. (*See* fig. 20.)

▼ *Fig. 19*

▼ *Fig. 20*

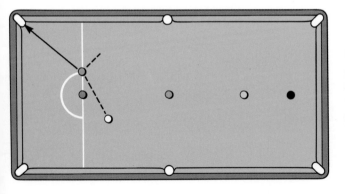

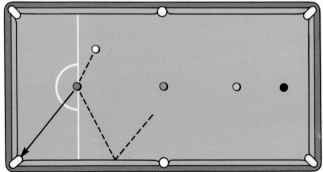

Blue

Play the three-quarter-ball contact as a plain ball run-through to leave a three-quarter-ball contact on the pink. (*See* fig. 21.)

Pink

Play the three-quarter-ball contact as a firm stun to leave a comfortable position on the black. (*See* fig. 22.)

▼ *Fig. 21*

▼ *Fig. 22*

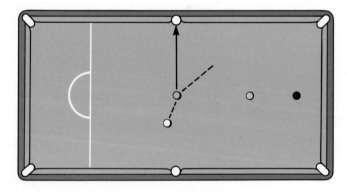

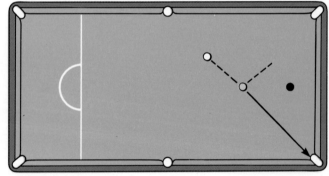

Black

Pot the black and, to all intents and purposes. the frame is over; unless of course the scores are level, in which case the black would be re-spotted and the next shot taken from baulk. (*See* fig. 23.)

It goes without saying that this is not the only method of clearing the colours. The most critical intention is to win the game. But the method shown is certainly easier than any alternative.

▼ *Fig. 23*

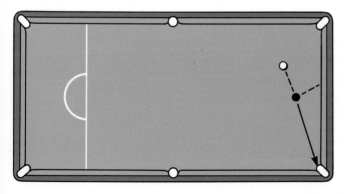

▲ *Keep your discipline!*

Terms of the table

Bed
The playing surface, consisting of five equal pieces of machined slate 1–3 in (3–8 cm) thick.

Frame of the table
All the woodwork appertaining to the table base.

Cushion rail
The outside wooden surface, in six parts, drilled to take the pocket plates.

Pocket plates
The pocket supports to which the leather and pocket nets are affixed. More modern tables have surface brass fittings fixed to the top of the cushion rails, and quite often the cushion rail is quite narrow. Invisible pocket plates are more recent and are concealed with a metal peg in the ends of the cushion rails.

Pocket leathers
The leather that is stitched and shaped on to the pocket plates at the impact point of the ball.

Pocket nets
Nets that act as the holding receptacle for the balls.

All games pockets
Pocket nets connected to runners allowing the balls to be retrieved without inserting the hand from the top (also known as 'Empire rails').

Cushion rubbers
The rubber strips that are glued on to the face of the cushion rails.

Cushion cloth
The cloth that covers the rubbers and is the same as the cloth on the playing surface.

Bed cloth
The cloth covering the playing surface.

Nap
The grain of the cloth which is fixed to the bed. The nap runs from the baulk end to the spot end.

Spots
The points on the cloth on which the various colours sit.

Pocket opening
The points where the balls enter the pocket.

Using the rest from a comfortable. ▶
well-balanced position

Glossary

Back-spin: the effect of striking the cue ball below centre.

Break: a sequence of scoring shots.

Break-off: the opening shot of a frame in which the striker must play at the triangle of reds.

Check side: side-spin that narrows the angle at which the cue ball rebounds from the cushion.

Clearance: a sequence of scoring shots continues until the player has potted all the balls left on the table.

'D': the semi-circle inscribed on the baulk line from which all strokes must be played when the striker is in hand, e.g. when breaking off.

Double: a shot by which the object ball is potted after striking one or more cushions.

Double kiss: a second contact on the object ball.

Drag shot: a long shot that is played with normal strength and plenty of back-spin, the effect being to slow down the cue ball late in its journey.

Fluke: a shot that results in a fortuitous bonus, e.g. an unintentional pot or snooker.

Forcing shot: a stroke played considerably above medium pace.

Foul stroke: a shot or action that infringes one of the rules of the game, thereby incurring a specified penalty.

Free ball: the result of a snooker caused by a foul stroke. The player snookered in this way (i.e. he cannot hit both extremities of the object ball) may nominate any coloured ball as a red for the purposes of his next shot. If he pots it he scores one, and then nominates a colour in the usual manner. If there are no reds left on the table, he nominates one of the colours as a free ball, and if he pots it he scores the value of the lowest value ball on the table. The nominated colour is re-spotted and he then plays the colours in sequence.

Full ball contact: striking the object ball full face, so that all of it is covered by the cue ball at the moment of impact.

Half-ball contact: striking the object ball so that half of it is covered by the cue ball at the moment of impact.

Half-butt: a matching 7.5 ft (2.3 m) cue and rest required to reach the cue ball for any shots too distant to reach with the normal rest.

In-off: a shot resulting in the cue ball being pocketed – a foul stroke.

Kick: an unclean contact between cue ball and object ball, caused by chalk, dust or anything that results in the de-glossing of a portion of one of the balls. It distorts the angle of deflection, and sometimes causes the cue ball to lift off slightly.

Kiss: contact by the cue ball on a second (or subsequent) object ball.

Massé: a shot in which the cue strikes almost vertically down on one side of the cue ball, imparting maximum swerve. It is much more common in billiards than snooker.

Maximum break: a scoring sequence in which the player pots all 15 reds, 15 blacks and all the colours to score a maximum total of 147.

Natural angle: the angle the cue ball will take after striking the object ball at medium pace without spin of any sort.

Plain ball: centre striking of the cue ball, i.e. no top-spin, back-spin or side.

Plant: a position in which one object ball is played on to another object ball in order to pot the latter.

Pocket weight: a slow shot carrying pace just sufficient to carry the object ball to the pocket.

Power shot: forcing shot of great pace.

Quarter-ball contact: striking the ball so that a quarter of it is covered by the cue ball at the moment of impact.

Rest: the smallest and least cumbersome of the implements used to reach the cue ball when it is beyond comfortable range for a conventional bridge.

Running side: side-spin that widens the angle at which the cue ball rebounds from the cushion.

▲ *Constantly think about your alignment*

Safe position: a lie from which a scoring strike is unlikely.

Safety shot: a defensive stroke that aims not to score but to leave the opponent in a safe position.

Screw: to impart back-spin to the cue ball, the result being a stun, screw or drag shot, depending on factors of distance and pace.

Screw shot: a shot in which the cue ball recoils from the object ball on contact (if full ball), or leaves it at wider than the natural angle if the contact is angled.

Set: a type of plant in which the two object balls are touching.

Shot to nothing: a tactical shot whereby the player attempts to pot the ball in such a way as to leave himself in a position to continue the break should he succeed with the pot, but leaving his opponent in a safe position should he fail.

Side-spin: referred to simply as 'side', the effect of striking the cue ball off centre (right or left). It will either widen or narrow the angle at which the cue ball rebounds from a cushion, and can be used in conjunction with either back-spin or top-spin.

Snooker: a lie from which the player is prevented from hitting both sides of the object ball by an intervening ball that is not on.

Spider: a rest with a raised head, allowing bridging at a distance over an intervening ball or balls. There are variations, devised for particularly awkward positions.

Stun shot: a shot in which the cue ball stops dead on contact with the object ball (if full ball), or leaves it at a wider than normal angle (but not as wide as a screw shot) if the contact is angled. Stun shots usually require the application of screw, but where the cue ball and object ball are very close together, stun may be achieved by central striking or even slightly higher.

Stun run-through shot: a shot at close quarters where the object is to retard the cue ball's forward momentum after contact with the object ball, but not kill it totally.

Swerve: the exaggerated side-spin achieved by striking down on one side of the cue ball, the object being to curve the cue ball around an obstructing ball.

Three-quarter-ball contact: striking the object ball so that three-quarters of it is covered by the cue ball at the moment of impact.

Three-quarter butt: a 9 ft (2.75 m) version of the half-butt, mercifully needed only rarely.

Top-spin: the effect achieved by striking the cue ball above centre.

Index